Horses Have Foals

by Lynn M. Stone

Animals and Their Young

Content Adviser: Terrence E. Young Jr., M.Ed., M.L.S.
Jefferson Parish (La.) Public Schools

Reading Adviser: Dr. Linda D. Labbo,
Department of Reading Education, College of Education,
The University of Georgia

COMPASS POINT BOOKS

Minneapolis, Minnesota

Compass Point Books
3722 West 50th Street, #115
Minneapolis, MN 55410

For more information about Compass Point Books, e-mail your request to:
custserv@compasspointbooks.com

Photographs ©: Lynn M. Stone, 4, 14, 16, 18, 20; Norvia Behling, 6, 8, 10; Paulette Johnson, 12

Editors: E. Russell Primm and Emily J. Dolbear
Photo Researcher: Svetlana Zhurkina
Photo Selector: Linda S. Koutris
Design: Bradfordesign, Inc.

Library of Congress Cataloging-in-Publication Data

Stone, Lynn M.
   Horses have foals / by Lynn Stone.
      p. cm. — (Animals and their young)
   Includes bibliographical references and index.
   Summary: Describes the appearance and behavior of foals from birth to six months.
   ISBN 0-7565-0002-8 (lib. bdg.)
     1. Foals—Juvenile literature. [1. Horses. 2. Animals—Infancy.] I. Title. II. Series:
Stone, Lynn M. Animals and their young.
SF302 .S764 2000
636.1'07—dc21
                                                        00-008832

Table of Contents

What Are Foals?

Baby horses are called foals. The mother horse is a **mare**. The father horse is a **stallion**.

A mare usually gives birth to only one foal at a time. It is unusual for a mare to have twins. Foals may be born at any time of the year.

◀ A foal rests by its mother.

How Do Foals Arrive?

A newborn foal is wet from being inside its mother's body. The mare licks her baby dry right away. Licking helps the mare and foal learn each other's smell. As the mare licks her foal, she nudges it. Her gentle push helps the foal stand up on its feet.

A foal has long legs. But a newborn foal's legs are wobbly. Those thin legs have to hold up a body that weighs 50 to 60 pounds (23 to 27 kilograms)! Yet, a newborn foal can usually stand up within thirty minutes after being born.

A foal walks on its thin legs.

How Do Foals Feed?

Newborn foals are born with certain **instincts**. They know how to do things without being taught. Instinct is one of nature's ways to help animals.

For example, a foal is born with the instinct to suck milk from its mother. Soon after it can stand, the foal finds its mother's milk. Drinking its mother's milk in this way is called **nursing**.

◀ A hungry foal drinks milk from its mother.

What Do Newborn Foals Do?

Most foals are born in barns or pens. A foal can run around soon after birth. With the mare nearby, the foal feels safe.

Mother's milk is the only food a newborn foal needs. It gives the foal energy.

Foals stay close to their mothers.

What Does a Foal Look Like?

A newborn foal's legs seem much too long for its body. In every other way, a foal is just a small form of its mother.

It has its mother's big, dark eyes and soft, silky nose. It also has its mother's smooth coat of hair. A young foal has the start of a **mane** and a long, flowing tail.

◀ Foals look like their mothers.

What Colors Are Foals?

A foal may or may not be the same color as its mother. Horses may be black, white, brown, creamy, gray, or spotted. If a foal's mother and father are the same color, the foal will probably be that color too.

Some foals change color as they grow older. The Lipizzan breed, or kind, of horse changes color as it grows older. Lipizzans are dark gray when they are born. Between the ages of four and ten, they become white!

Sometimes foals aren't the same color as their mothers.

What Do Foals Do and Eat?

A newborn foal stays close to its mother. It nurses or sleeps most of the time. But by the time the foal is a week old, it is taken out of the **stable**.

Horse owners like to **lead** new foals as soon as they can. They want the foals to get used to being around people. They also want the foal to learn that a person is not a horse.

Once outside, playful foals exercise with their mothers. A foal's day is much like its mother's day. When the mother runs, her foal runs at her side.

◄ A young horse owner feeds her foal.

What Happens As a Foal Grows Older?

Newborn foals pick at their mother's dry food right away. They don't eat much of it, however. Some foals don't even have teeth for the first few days.

Soon foals begin eating special food called pellets. They eat the pellets for about a year. Then, they eat more grain and grassy hay.

When a foal is three to six months old, it stops drinking its mother's milk. Then it eats only solid foods.

As a foal gets older, it eats grass and solid food.

When Is a Foal Grown Up?

Young horses love to run and sometimes kick their heels up. Young male horses rear up on their hind legs and strike out with their front legs.

Most breeds of horses stop growing when they are five or six years old. Some horses, however, are big and strong enough to carry a rider when they are only two years old.

A young mare does not usually give birth to a foal until she is about four years old. She and her foal could live twenty-five or thirty years.

◀ Young horses are full of energy!

Glossary

instincts—knowing what to do without being taught; natural behaviors

lead—to follow a person who guides the foal with a strap

mane—the long hair on the neck of a horse

mare—an adult female horse; a mother horse

nursing—drinking milk produced by the mother

stable—a building where farm animals live

stallion—an adult male horse; a father horse

Did You Know?

- Horses were first used by humans more than 6,000 years ago.

- More than 60 million horses are kept by people around the world.

- Horses have the largest eyes of any mammal on land.

Want to Know More?

At the Library
Burton, Jane. *Pacer, the Pony*. New York: Random House, 1989.

Clayton, Gordon. *Foal*. New York: Dorling Kindersley, 1992.

Patent, Dorothy Hinshaw. *Baby Horses*. Minneapolis: Carolrhoda Books, 1991.

On the Web
Horse Fun

http://horsefun.com/index.html

For contests, puzzles, and games for the horse lover

Through the Mail
Adopt-a-Horse Program

Bureau of Land Management

U.S. Department of the Interior

P.O. Box 12000

Reno, NV 89520

For information on how to adopt wild horses and burros

On the Road
The International Museum of the Horse

Kentucky Horse Park

4089 Iron Works Parkway

Lexington, KY 40511

http://www.imh.org/imh/imhmain.html

This museum is a part of a working horse farm that covers 1,032 acres (418 hectares). It shows the 6,000-year relationship between humans and horses.

Index

About the Author

Lynn M. Stone has written hundreds of children's books and many articles on natural history for various magazines. He has photographed wildlife and domestic animals on all seven continents for such magazines as *National Geographic, Time, Ranger Rick, Natural History, Field and Stream*, and *Audubon*.

Lynn Stone earned a bachelor's degree at Aurora University in Illinois and a master's degree at Northern Illinois University. He taught in the West Aurora schools for several years before becoming a writer-photographer full-time. He lives with his wife and daughter in Batavia, Illinois.